BEYOND COMPLIANCE, INTO COMMAND

A Manifesto for Company Secretaries to Lead with ***Law, Ethics,*** and ***Strategy***

BEYOND COMPLIANCE, INTO COMMAND

A Manifesto for Company Secretaries
to Lead with ***Law, Ethics,*** and ***Strategy***

CS Dikshant Malhotra

Available on amazonkindle

Worldwide Published by

Pendown Press
PREMIUM BUSINESS PUBLISHER

PENDOWN PRESS LLP

An ISO 9001 & ISO 14001 Certified Co.,

Regd. Office: 3767A, Kanhaiya Nagar,
Tri Nagar, Delhi-110035
Ph.: 8130886000, 9650072927, 8595249536
E-mail: info@pendownpress.com
Branch Office: 1A/2A, 20, Hari Sadan, Ansari Road,
Daryaganj, New Delhi-110002
Ph.: 011-45794768
Website: PendownPress.com

Edition: 2025
Price: ₹ 399
ISBN: 978-93-7217-014-6

Layout and Cover Designed by Pendown Graphics Team
Printed and Bound in India by Thomson Press India Ltd.

DEDICATION

To the unsung warriors of corporate India—

The Company Secretaries who work behind the scenes, not for the spotlight, but for integrity, governance, and truth.

To my parents, for instilling in me the values of discipline, ethics, and courage.

To Divya, my partner in every sense, for your love, strength, and unwavering faith.

And to little Dhriti—my greatest teacher in patience, hope, and purpose.

This is not just a book.

- It's a movement.
- A tribute.
- A beginning.

A PROFESSIONAL DISCLAIMER

The content of this book, *"Beyond Compliance into Command,"* is intended for informational and educational purposes only. While every effort has been made to ensure the accuracy of the legal, regulatory, and strategic insights shared, this book does not constitute professional, legal, or financial advice.

Readers are advised to consult a qualified professional or legal advisor before acting on any information provided herein. The author, contributors, and publisher disclaim any liability for loss, damage, or legal consequences incurred as a result of reliance on the material presented.

All case studies, examples, and scenarios used in this book—unless otherwise indicated—are fictional or anonymized composites created for illustrative purposes. Any resemblance to real individuals, companies, or events is purely coincidental.

This book does not represent the views of any specific organization, regulatory body, or employer.

TABLE OF CONTENTS

PREFACE
A PROFESSION THE WORLD IS YET TO FULLY UNDERSTAND

Have you ever introduced yourself as a Company Secretary, only to be met with confusion or a dismissive nod?

Maybe someone even assumed you booked meetings or managed files.

We've all experienced those moments when a title respected in boardrooms seems trivialized in casual conversations.

But here's the truth the world needs to recognize:

We are the silent force keeping the corporate ship steady. You are the ethical spine, compliance conscience, and governance guide in an era of increasing complexity.

And it's time we proudly proclaim this.

This book exists with one clear intention: to shift this narrative, one page at a time.

Why This Book Exists

The role of a Company Secretary is rapidly evolving, yet public perception remains stuck in outdated stereotypes of paperwork, filings, and formalities.

The reality?

We are enablers of integrity, protectors of transparency, and architects of good governance.

Yet, few understand or articulate this clearly.

This book honors our professional journey-the challenges, values, and triumphs that shape us in a relatable voice, like a conversation between peers over coffee after a challenging compliance season.

This book is part tribute, part guidebook, and part manifesto:

- A tribute to our profession.
- A practical guide to our roles and responsibilities.
- A manifesto for our collective future.

What This Book Offers You

In the chapters ahead, you will discover:

- Authentic stories of Company Secretaries navigating ethical storms.
- Clear insights into compliance, governance, law, and leadership, presented in accessible language.
- Practical frameworks beyond mere theory.
- Inspiration drawn from professionals who've faced real-world challenges.
- A renewed sense of purpose and pride in our profession.

Whether you're a student preparing for exams, an employed Company Secretary guiding corporate governance, or a practising professional managing your consultancy, this book is designed for you.

If you've ever questioned whether your role matters, let this be your unequivocal answer: it absolutely does.

Company Secretaries: Guardians in the Shadows

Behind every ethically run company stands a Company Secretary who:

- Identified a critical governance issue overlooked by others.
- Prevented a compliance breach just in time.
- Clarified a board resolution to ensure legal soundness.
- Advocated against tempting shortcuts, championing long-term integrity.

Such vital work often happens quietly, unnoticed by the public.

Boards celebrate profits, and investors applaud growth, but beneath these successes is a Company Secretary ensuring each step is compliant, sustainable, and legally sound.

We may not always stand in the spotlight-but we certainly direct it toward what is right.

Living Our Motto: *"Satyam Vada, Dharmam Chara"*

At our profession's core is timeless wisdom from the Taittiriya Upanishad:

"Speak the Truth. Abide by the Law."

More than a motto, it's our guiding principle, a commitment that prompts us to act with integrity when others hesitate or look away.

This ancient wisdom, proudly embraced by the Institute of Company Secretaries of India (ICSI), distinguishes our profession.

It's the silent pledge each Company Secretary makes not only to their organization but also to their conscience.

The Ethical Spine of Corporate India

If a company is a body, we are its spine: essential for balance, posture, and strength, though often invisible.

We enable companies to stand firm amidst regulatory changes, ethical complexities, and commercial pressures. When tempting shortcuts arise, we're the voice asking, "It's legal, but is it ethical?" When transparency feels inconvenient, we're the ones advocating, "Let's do it right, openly and honestly."

That is leadership. That is governance. That is the daily commitment of Company Secretaries.

Recognition of Our Professional Milestones

We've made significant strides:

- Recognized as Key Managerial Personnel under the Companies Act, 2013.
- First country to adopt Secretarial Standards, spearheaded by the ICSI.
- Practising Company Secretaries are now authorized for critical filings and audits.
- ICSI's international presence expands our global influence.
- National Governance Awards highlighting our substantial contributions.

These achievements are collective milestones-our legacy. Every compliance signed, every meeting effectively managed, and every ethical decision made is proof of our indispensable role.

Voices from Our Community

Hear it directly from our peers:

"When I became a Company Secretary, I was told **I'd be the company's conscience**. It **felt abstract** until I **stood up against a legally dubious decision by a powerful board member**. **That's when I truly became a Company Secretary.**"

- Pooja, Company Secretary in Employment

"Clients rarely see the value of governance until something goes wrong. That's when we demonstrate the importance of doing things right from the start."

- Surya Prakash Parekh, Practising Company Secretary

These reflections capture the essence of our shared truths.

A Profession for All Stages:
Students, Practitioners, Employees

This book celebrates every segment of our community:

- **Company Secretary Students**: You are already part of our profession's journey.
- **Company Secretaries in Employment:** You carry the governance torch, balancing company Secretary and business.
- **Practising Company Secretaries**: You serve as trusted advisors, compliance experts, and industry guides.

Each role is significant. Each member is vital. Each holds the same profound responsibility to uphold trust, legality, and leadership.

What Lies Ahead

In this book, you will encounter:

- Comprehensive insights into compliance, governance, and strategic influence.
- Stories of courage and critical decision-making.
- Practical frameworks for navigating real-world challenges.
- Reflections on technology, ethics, leadership, and professional growth.
- Experiences shared by colleagues from boardrooms to startups, veterans to newcomers.

Consider this book your mirror, your guidebook, and your badge of honor.

A Personal Note from the Author

As someone who has spent over a decade advising startups, managing complex corporate structures, conducting board meetings, handling regulatory filings, and steering through demanding audits, I've personally walked this path.

I've experienced stressful days, deadline-driven nights, and moments of professional doubt. Yet, I've also known the profound satisfaction of guiding organizations to ethical choices-decisions that mattered profoundly, even if quietly.

That's our true power.

That's the pride we must confidently reclaim.

A Journey of Purpose and Discovery

Before we move on, I am sure you have understood that I am one of you, but you are curious to know who exactly I am and the journey that led me here.

My journey began not in boardrooms but in the lively classrooms of Delhi University, where I earned my Bachelor's in Commerce, filled with youthful dreams and aspirations. Initially, my professional path unfolded like many others, driven by ambition and a clear goal: to excel professionally and make a meaningful contribution.

However, my journey was far from linear.

Early in my career, while pursuing my qualifications as a Company Secretary, I experienced firsthand the complexities and intricacies of corporate governance, compliance, and ethical leadership.

The more I delved into the world of corporate governance, the deeper my passion grew-not just for the role of a Company Secretary, but for the larger purpose of meaningful corporate contribution and ethical leadership.

My professional experiences soon extended beyond compliance and governance. I founded Dikshant Malhotra & Associates, driven by a mission to create a practice built on trust, excellence, and a deep commitment to supporting businesses. Over the last decade, my firm has blossomed, and today it stands proudly as a testament to the power of integrity, collaboration, and focused determination.

But my journey wasn't limited to professional milestones alone. Alongside my career, I have always sought growth through personal exploration and self-discovery. My fascination with meditation, mindfulness, and energy sciences led me to the Art of Living Advanced Meditation Retreat, a transformative experience that profoundly impacted my outlook on life, relationships, and professional responsibilities. Becoming a father further enriched my life, offering invaluable lessons about patience, empathy, and purpose that deeply influenced my interactions and professional approach.

Today, my vision goes beyond just professional success. I actively strive to foster a sense of belonging and likeability within the professional community, sharing my learnings openly and creating opportunities for meaningful conversations. My mission has become clear: to uplift, inspire, and empower professionals and individuals alike, guiding them towards both professional excellence and personal fulfillment.

Writing this book, *Beyond Compliance Into Command*, is a culmination of all my personal and professional insights. Through my story, I aspire to connect with others on their own journeys, reminding us all that our true potential lies not only in professional achievement but in the personal growth and purposeful living we choose every day.

My story is not just about me-it's about each one of us, about discovering our purpose, and about building a community rooted in authenticity, excellence, and compassion.

CHAPTER 1

FROM COMPLIANCE CUSTODIAN TO STRATEGIC KMP

Imagine being legally placed shoulder-to-shoulder with the CEO and CFO as a key managerial force. That's precisely where the Companies Act, 2013 positions Company Secretaries today.

For the first time in Indian corporate law, Section 203 of the Companies Act, 2013, formally included the Company Secretary in the definition of Key Managerial Personnel (KMP). This recognition is not symbolic-it is structural. It bestows power, voice, and accountability in equal measure.

This shift transformed Company Secretaries from being mere custodians of minutes to guardians of corporate conscience. As a KMP, your role extends beyond filings into influencing strategy, championing ethical conduct, and guiding the boardroom through legal complexities.

The Act expects you to:

- Certify compliance with all applicable laws
- Ensure adherence to Secretarial Standards
- Report lapses and enforce accountability
- Support the Board in aligning business decisions with legal frameworks

And with these responsibilities comes liability. You are now legally considered an "officer in default" under Section 2(60), which means that **if the company breaches key provisions, you can be held personally liable.**

At first glance, this may seem burdensome. But **in reality, it is a professional privilege-a badge of trust. It means your voice matters. Your legal opinion shapes business behavior. Your signature carries institutional weight.**

This elevated legal position has practical implications. Company Secretaries are now expected **not just to 'ensure compliance' but to actively design, monitor, and continuously improve the compliance systems within an organization.** You are a change agent-transforming law into strategy and governance into culture. When companies are recognized for integrity, chances are an ethical and insightful Company Secretary stands behind that reputation.

A Trusted Advisor (A KMP)

Not Merely A Compliance Expert

"When our startup hit a roadblock due to a founders' dispute, **everything was at stake — investor confidence, team morale, and future growth**. That's **when CS Dikshant Malhotra stepped in**.

With calm authority and deep legal insight, he guided us through a structured, lawful exit strategy that protected the company and preserved relationships.

His strategic thinking, balanced counsel, and mastery of corporate law turned a crisis into clarity.

More than a compliance expert, he was our trusted advisor when it mattered most."

Director – Pvt Ltd. Group

Let's explore a day in the life of two Company Secretaries to better understand the modern scope of this role.

Meet Radhika: The In-House Company Secretary

At 9:00 AM, she's reviewing a new MCA circular on e-form filing updates.

By 10:00 AM, she's briefing the compliance team, updating timelines, and responding to queries from internal stakeholders.

By noon, she's coordinating with auditors, updating statutory registers, preparing Board packs, and advising on director disclosures. During the Board meeting, **she isn't just a note-taker; she's the legal compass in the room.**

Post-lunch, she's acting as the SEBI-designated Compliance Officer-drafting investor responses, coordinating disclosures to stock exchanges, and reviewing the conclusion of the meeting

By 6:00 PM, she's still at her desk, cross-verifying everything thoroughly & diligently

Her work never really ends because governance never sleeps.

Also Meet Yogita Bhatia: The Practising Company Secretary

Her day begins with a client call-a startup planning to issue shares to a foreign investor.

Within hours, she's interpreting FEMA guidelines, reviewing sectoral caps, and mapping out the FC-GPR filing process.

By midday, she's on-site at a manufacturing client's office for a Secretarial Audit. She spots a pending ECB compliance issue and escalates it, **avoiding a possible RBI penalty.**

By evening, she's leading a virtual workshop on Startup compliance for early-stage founders. She wears the hats of consultant, educator, and watchdog & sometimes all at once.

Different contexts. Same purpose. Both Radhika and Yogita protect businesses by empowering them to do what's right.

These scenarios reflect the depth of knowledge modern Company Secretaries must embody-legal, Secretarial, technological, interpersonal, and strategic. More importantly, they reflect the human side of the profession, empathy, ethiCompany Secretary, and the resolve to stand firm when it matters most.

Domain Mastery: Where the Company Secretary Makes a Difference

Modern Company Secretaries are legal navigators across a vast regulatory terrain:

Companies Act, 2013

From incorporation to board governance, director appointments to audits, the Company Secretary ensures nothing slips through the cracks. Secretarial Standards (SS-1, SS-2), statutory registers, e-forms, resolutions- this is your playground. You are the reason the company avoids late filings, penalty notices, or shareholder disputes.

SEBI and Capital Market Compliance

As the designated Compliance Officer under SEBI's LODR Regulations, your role in listed companies is mission-critical. You oversee insider trading policies, ensure timely disclosures, advise the Board on governance norms, and manage investor relations-all while safeguarding the company's public reputation.

FEMA, FDI, and ECB

From FC-GPR filings to external commercial borrowings, you ensure cross-border capital flows are structured, reported, and compliant. You are the bridge between foreign investors, authorized dealers, and regulators. A missed FEMA filing can cost crores. Your vigilance can prevent that.

ESG, CSR, and Beyond

You are increasingly guiding Boards through ESG frameworks, CSR policy implementation, and Business Responsibility and Sustainability Reporting (BRSR). Your influence ensures that sustainability and ethical accountability become strategic imperatives.

Across all these domains, you do more than manage risk-you build trust. Your insight enables businesses to operate ethically in a complex, ever-changing world. And in doing so, you earn your seat at the leadership table.

A Company Secretary's Skill & Commitment Deflects A Huge Penalty

A Caselet

Meet Divya, Company Secretary of a Unicorn Startup. They had just secured ₹100 crore in foreign investment.

Everyone celebrated-except no one filed the FC-GPR form.

When Divya returned from leave, only five days remained before the 30-day filing deadline.

She sprang into action-coordinating with bankers, retrieving valuation reports, organizing Board resolutions, **and submitting the filing on Day 29.**

Had she missed it, the company faced a hefty RBI penalty.

Her timely intervention saved not just money, but the company's regulatory goodwill.

The Chairman later said:

"We almost dropped the ball, but our Company Secretary caught it mid-air."

This isn't just a story-it's a reminder:

What Company Secretary professionals prevent is just as important as what they do.

Company Secretary in Employment vs. Practising Company Secretary: Two Paths, One Purpose

➢ **Company Secretary in Employment**

You are embedded in the organization. You advise, execute, and influence decisions from the inside out. You align internal processes with external obligations.

- **Practising Company Secretary (PCS)**

  You are an external expert. You consult, audit, certify, and guide multiple entities across sectors. You offer perspective, independence, and legal precision.

Despite their differences, both roles require:

- Legal mastery
- Fearless communication
- Ethical clarity
- Strategic vision

Together, they form the checks and balances that uphold corporate integrity.

The Company Secretary Value Proposition in 2025

Future-Ready, Ethics-Led

Role	What It Looks Like
Compliance Champion	Ensuring regulatory precision in a sea of filings and laws
Tech-Enabled Leader	Managing governance through digital tools, AI systems, and cloud platforms
ESG Strategist	Aligning the company with sustainable and ethical impact goals
Boardroom Influencer	Advising on business risks, legal implications, and ethical considerations
Culture Builder	Promoting transparency, fairness, and accountability from the top down
Lifelong Learner	Continuously adapting, upskilling, and staying ahead of emerging regulations

You're not just keeping companies out of trouble, you're shaping how business is done: **ethically, efficiently, and intelligently.**

You, the Company Secretary, are no longer on the sidelines. You are at the center of compliance, governance, and decision-making.

Honouring The Multi-Functional Impact of Company Secretaries

"Behind every seamless AGM, every timely disclosure, and every confident boardroom decision, there's a Company Secretary orchestrating it all.

Our in-house CS ensures we stay ahead of regulatory expectations, while **our Practising CS partners bring an external lens that keeps us sharper** and more accountable. Together, they form the compliance backbone that protects our reputation and powers our governance engine. **This book captures their pivotal role with both clarity and heart."**

CEO- Listed Company

From technology to ethiCompany Secretary, sustainability to legal design, your world is evolving. And it is your insight, discipline, and integrity that help organizations navigate the future.

So, the next time someone asks what a Company Secretary really does, tell them:

"I keep businesses ethical. I keep decisions lawful. And I keep the Board accountable. I'm a Company Secretary - and proud of it."

Chapter 2

Desires and Challenges of the Company Secretary

A Mirror Morning: Priya And The AGM

It was 5:30 AM when Priya, a seasoned Company Secretary in a mid-sized listed company, brewed her first cup of tea. **Today was her company's Annual General Meeting**-an event she had orchestrated many times, yet each year **felt like walking a tightrope without a net.**

Her mental checklist ticked away: agenda vetted, statutory registers updated, proxy forms accounted for, compliance documentation ready. **The Chairman's speech? Drafted,** reviewed, rehearsed. **Directors briefed. Shareholder questions anticipated.**

Her mentor's words echoed in her mind:

> ***"The Company Secretary is the guardian behind the scenes. Prepare so well that the Board shines effortlessly."***

By 7:45 AM, Priya was at the office, greeting her team. They had worked tirelessly over the past few weeks, driven by one principle she always repeated: "Systems protect you under pressure."

But real-world execution rarely sticks to scripts. **A director had misplaced his disclosure.** A **shareholder demanded clarification** on a related party transaction. **The Chairman was suddenly unsure about a legal nuance in the agenda.**

Priya addressed each curveball with quiet authority. No panic. Just practiced presence.

As the AGM began, she moved through the boardroom like a conductor-keeping every section in tune.

A late-arriving shareholder's proxy issue? Handled.

An obscure investor query? Answered with grace.

She directed the flow between the Board and shareholders-without ever taking center stage.

And yet, **when applause echoed for the Chairman and CFO, Priya wondered** in the hallway silence:

Will anyone ever truly know the depth of what I did today?

Priya's story isn't fiction. It's a reflection-a mirror held up to the lived truth of thousands of Company Secretaries across India.

Professional sentinels who carry the weight of compliance, the nerves of risk, and the hope of impact. Unthanked, but never uncommitted.

Beneath the Surface: What Today's Company Secretaries Really Desire

Today's Company Secretaries are more than compliance officers. They are educators, strategists, confidants, and guardians. And behind their day-to-day responsibilities lies a deeper longing for contribution, transformation, and meaningful recognition.

They desire:

- **Recognition as Strategic Allies**: Company Secretaries want to be seen not as documentation gatekeepers but as advisors shaping ethical decisions and mitigating enterprise risk.
- **Growth Beyond Compliance**: Many aspire to lead ESG initiatives, advise on M&A structuring, and contribute to startup ecosystems.
- **Work-Life Alignment**: Balancing board meetings and family dinners is a daily challenge. Company Secretaries crave room for personal growth without guilt.
- **Mentorship and Mobility:** With the right exposure, they see a future in COO, CFO, and even CEO roles.
- **Purpose-Driven Work**: They want their role to reflect their calling to build businesses that last, ethically and legally.

"I didn't become a Company Secretary to just file eForms. I became one to shape the legal conscience of a business."

"Let us in the room where vision is discussed, not just where decisions are documented."

"The law isn't a hurdle. It's the framework that builds sustainable companies."

These are some of the sentiments that arise within Company Secretaries.

Unseen Battles: The Real Challenges They Face

Behind every aspiration is a challenge, often silent, often misunderstood. The life of a Company Secretary is filled with paradoxes: influence without visibility, responsibility without applause, pressure without pause.

1. **The Weight of Invisible Pressure**
   - Company Secretaries are the final checkpoint before a mistake becomes a penalty or litigation.
   - A single missed deadline or clause can have cascading consequences.
   - The expectation of 100% precision leaves little space for rest or error.
2. **The Boardroom Illusion**
   - Company Secretaries prepare the agenda, anticipate risks, and vet documents-yet are rarely invited to strategic dialogue.
   - Governance wins are deemed "routine," while financial wins get celebrated.
   - **A deep asymmetry persists:** Company Secretaries understand business; few business leaders fully understand Company Secretaries.
3. **The Isolation of Responsibility**
   - Many Company Secretaries work solo or in lean teams, especially in smaller firms or consultancies.
   - Unlike CFOs or CHROs, they lack in-house peers to brainstorm with.
   - In practice, clients view them more as service providers than strategic partners.
4. **The Tsunami of Legal Change**
   - From Companies Act amendments to SEBI LODR, FEMA, ESG reporting-change is constant.
   - They must interpret, implement, and train others-often with no buffer.
   - Company Secretaries don't specialize-they synchronize across MCA, SEBI, RBI, Labour, Tax, and more.

5. **Limited Tech Support**
   - Tools exist-but are underfunded and underused.
   - The burden of tracking due dates, drafting notices, and coordinating filings often remains manual.

The Desire–Challenge Dilemma

Desires	Challenges
Strategic boardroom presence	Treated as post-facto legal validators
Influence over corporate direction	Limited access to decision-making forums
Legal mastery and foresight	Constantly evolving regulations
Meaningful work-life blend	24×7 readiness expectation
Respect as governance experts	Seen as operational executors
Growth beyond the Company Secretary role	Narrow perception of contribution

What the Data Says (and Doesn't Say Out Loud)

One survey revealed

- 67% feel under-recognized by senior leadership
- 74% report high stress at least once a week
- Only 18% believe their governance input shapes Board decisions
- 83% want access to leadership mentoring programs
- 51% of practising Company Secretaries say clients treat them like vendors, not advisors

These aren't signals of weakness; they're symptoms of underutilization. And yet, Company Secretaries continue their work with dignity, discipline, and dedication.

From Overlooked to Empowered: The Toolkit Preview

This book is more than a reflection; it's a roadmap. In the coming chapters, we'll unlock:

- Companies Act strategies for leadership, not just compliance
- How to influence Boardroom dialogue without a formal title
- Real stories of Company Secretaries building trust, driving culture, and earning influence
- Practical ways to shift from executor to advisor
- How to leverage tech, community, and content to reclaim your power

This isn't a theory. It's a lived insight. Proven. Practiced. Possible.

Where You Stand and Where You Can Rise

If you've ever felt unseen, overworked, or misunderstood are not alone.

You chose this profession not just for a paycheck-but for a purpose: governance, law, order, and service.

The world may not always see it. But this book does. And it is written for you.

You are more than a compliance function. You are the voice of governance when no one else is listening.

CHAPTER 3

FROM BACK OFFICE TO BOARDROOM: BREAKING THE STEREOTYPE

"You are not just a compliance officer; you are the conscience of governance."

A Role Reimagined

For years, the Company Secretary was cast in the shadows, a legal mind ticking boxes, preparing registers, and quietly drafting minutes. Often seen as the "compliance guy" or "minutes taker," Company Secretaries were responsible for keeping companies on the right side of the law, but rarely invited to shape their future.

But today, a quiet revolution is underway in boardrooms across India.

- **Company Secretaries are stepping out of the stereotypical back office** and emerging as strategic advisors, ethical stewards, and governance leaders.
- **No longer confined to filings and checklists, they are influencing ESG agendas**, navigating enterprise risk, driving digital transformation, and shaping a company's public narrative.

How did this transformation begin-and more importantly, **how can you accelerate it in your own journey?**

This chapter explores the evolution of the Company Secretary role and **offers a roadmap to transition from compliance caretakers to governance strategists.**

Catalysts of Change

The shift wasn't accidental. It was born of necessity and seized as an opportunity.

In the past decade, corporate governance has undergone seismic shifts. Regulatory complexity has skyrocketed. Stakeholder scrutiny has intensified. Ethical behavior and transparency are now non-negotiable.

From the Companies Act to SEBI regulations, RBI norms, and ESG frameworks-compliance today is no longer a department. It is a culture.

Company Secretaries, positioned at the intersection of legal, financial, and boardroom affairs, were uniquely equipped to navigate this complexity. Some seized the moment. They initiated governance conversations, educated the board, and took charge of issues beyond statutory checklists.

Take the ESG movement. As investor and regulatory pressure mounted, many companies lacked a clear ESG lead. Enter the Company Secretary-respected in the boardroom, proficient in documentation, and fluent in legal requirements. Many stepped in to lead ESG committees, embed sustainability into strategy, and steer internal reporting frameworks.

This wasn't just compliance. It was leadership.

Tarun's Story: The Governance Crusader

Tarun is the Company Secretary at a **leading digital media company**

Reliable, efficient…

When CSR, ethics, and governance took center stage, Tarun saw an opportunity.

He started attending webinars, reading global reports, and sharing short, sharp governance insights with the board.

Then he took a bold step, saying:
"Let's form a Governance & Ethics Committee."

The leadership hesitated, but Tarun explained how it builds trust and reduces risk. They agreed.

Soon, he began sending quarterly newsletters—no legal jargon, just trends, case studies, and big-picture thinking.

During one meeting on ESG disclosures, the Chairman turned to him and asked,

"Tarun, what do you think?"

That question changes everything.

Today, Tarun leads governance and sustainability conversations at the company.

Not because his role changed, **but because he chose to lead.**

The Strategic Shift: What It Takes

1. **Showcase Broader Value**

   Boards and CXOs often don't grasp the full breadth of a Company Secretary's capabilities. **It's your responsibility to illustrate it-not by explaining, but by demonstrating.**

   After an AGM or regulatory success, don't just report: "All filings completed."

   Instead, say: "Filed 3 days ahead of deadline, saving ₹3.5 lakh in penalties and safeguarding director liability."

   Translate legal compliance into business value.

2. **Volunteer for Strategic Initiatives**

   Leadership isn't assigned-it's assumed.

   Step up for cross-functional initiatives: GDPR rollouts, whistleblower systems, digital policy training, ESG reporting, or sustainability audits. **Collaborate with IT, HR, or Marketing**. Projects like these give you visibility and multi-disciplinary exposure.

3. **Break the 'Minutes-Taker' Mold**

   Minute writing is vital-but it must not define you.

   Use the boardroom proactively:

   - Shape the agenda with forward-looking governance topics
   - Offer context during legal queries
   - Create one-pagers simplifying regulatory changes
   - Send post-meeting action briefs connecting decisions to business implications

   Become known for insight-not just accuracy.

4. **Build Trust at the Top**

   Strategic access is built on strategic trust. With CEOs, CFOs, and Board Chairs:

   - Be consistent: deliver reliably
   - Be discreet: handle sensitive matters with maturity
   - Be competent: bring domain mastery and current awareness

   Understand their pressures. **Offer insight-not just tasks.** Trust opens doors that designations cannot.

5. **Adopt the Strategic Mindset**

   Before others see you as a leader-you must see yourself as one.

   When you internalize that belief, your language, posture, and energy change. You ask sharper questions. You connect your work to purpose. You advocate boldly.

   "When you think of yourself as a leader, the board starts seeing you as one too."

Voices from the Field: Insights and Aspirations

➢ **"The rules change faster than we can read them!"**

In 2024 alone, India saw 9,331 compliance updates-about 42 per day. Vacations feel like risk accumulation.

➢ **"We're still treated as form-fillers."**

60% of Company Secretaries in a LinkedIn poll said they want greater strategic recognition. "We understand governance and strategy-yet we're often consulted last."

"We're guardians-not jailbirds."

- **"Our Company Secretary keeps us honest and forward-thinking."**

  A conglomerate's board member shared: "He's in every strategic meeting-not just for legalities, but for perspective."

  "We must upskill constantly."

- **A 2023 survey showed 40% of members aspire to C-suite roles.**

Barriers? Recognition, burnout, and personal branding.

Your Strategic Growth Toolkit

Growth Area	Action Step
Lifelong Learning	Block 1 hour/week for updates. Follow the ICSI, SEBI, and MCA portals.
Tech Proficiency	Learn 1 tool/quarter (Trello, Excel macros, XBRL, Notion, Asana).
Financial Acumen	Sit with Finance during closures. Learn ratios. Analyze quarterly reports.
Communication Skills	Join Toastmasters. Post explainers on LinkedIn. Seek feedback on emails & memos.
Personal Branding	Attend ICSI events. Speak on panels. Publish blog posts. Build your voice online.
Leadership	Mentor juniors. Lead internal training. Volunteer for strategic committees.
Time & Energy	Use time blocks, take breaks, and plan priorities. Avoid burnout.
Ethical Backbone	Speak truth with grace. Say no with strength. Protect the company's conscience.

The Time to Step Up is NOW!

This is your time.

Whether you're an assistant Company Secretary, a solo practitioner, or a seasoned professional, you have the power to reshape perception.

Step into the light. Raise your hand. Ask the bold question. Share your insight. Publish that post.

The Company Secretary of tomorrow is not just compliant-they are commanding.

"The Company Secretary profession is not a sprint, but a marathon with hurdles. Every hurdle crossed makes you stronger and more respected. Enjoy the run."

Here's to your rise as a strategic partner in governance-and to the legacy you will build.

CHAPTER 4

GUARDIANS OF GOVERNANCE – TECHNICAL EXCELLENCE WITH HEART

How Company Secretaries Turn Meetings into Milestones and Compliancc into Trust

A Board Meeting Done Right!

A soft morning light filters into the boardroom as Riya, the Company Secretary of a Tech Company, takes her seat. **Today's board meeting isn't just routine - it's pivotal. The company will decide whether to make its first move into overseas markets.**

There's a quiet gravity in the air. But **Riya, backed by weeks of strategic prep, is calm. Composed. Ready.**

Seven days earlier, she had circulated the board meeting notice and agenda, but not just the minimum. **Each item came with background notes, legal references, financial implications, and strategic context. The directors walked in, informed, thanks to her.**

She also took the time to personally onboard a new independent director - explaining the business model, board dynamiCompany Secretary, and company culture.

Her foresight turned a procedural meeting into a purposeful one.

As the meeting commenced, Riya stayed behind the scenes - but fully in control. Every register updated. Every step checked. She scanned the room, always a moment ahead.

When a legal question about joint venture structuring arose, Riya calmly referenced the Companies Act and SEBI guidelines, citing provisions clearly and confidently.

Later, when an aggressive expansion proposal surfaced, Riya raised an eyebrow subtly. The Chairman noticed and paused. That moment opened space for reflection. A better, more aligned path emerged.

By the end, the Chairman remarked, "Thanks to our Company Secretary's foresight and preparation, we navigated a complex agenda with ease."

Behind Riya's calm confidence was a landscape of technical mastery -

The silent scaffolding that holds board decisions upright.

As others left, Riya stayed back - annotating decisions, organizing resolutions, preparing disclosures.

She wasn't just documenting outcomes - she was shaping the future.

Pillar 1: Mastering Statutory Compliance (Companies Act + SEBI Essentials)

The Legal Backbone of Trust

A Company Secretary is not just a rule-follower. They are the professional conscience of the company.

This begins with two pillars:

- **The Companies Act, 2013**
- **SEBI (LODR) Regulations, 2015**

Section 205 of the Companies Act places a statutory duty on the Company Secretary to report to the board about legal compliance. Every agenda, filing, and register must be accurate, timely, and traceable.

Under SEBI LODR Regulation 6, the Company Secretary of a listed company becomes the designated Compliance Officer. Their role: ensure full conformity in letter and spirit, verify disclosures, and act as a regulatory bridge.

This is where the Company Secretary transforms from compliance manager to trust enabler.

Top 10 Statutory Hotspots Company Secretaries Must Master

1. Board Meetings & Resolutions (Sec. 173, SS-1)
2. Director Disclosures & Registers (Sec. 184, 189)
3. Filing Accuracy & Timeliness (MGT-7, AOC-4, PAS-3, DIR-12)
4. Secretarial Audit (Sec. 204, Reg. 24A)
5. SEBI LODR Disclosures & Compliance Certificates
6. Board Composition & Governance Reports
7. Dividend Decisions & Solvency Checks (Sec. 123)
8. Investor Grievance Mechanism Oversight

9. Annual Return Certification (Sec. 92)

10. Vigil Mechanism & Whistleblower Policies

> ***"The Company Secretary is often the company's first line of governance - and its last line of trust."***

Seasoned Company Secretaries guide decision-making, manage risk, and protect reputation. In their world, accuracy is integrity.

Pillar 2: Leading Governance Culture in the Boardroom

The Gatekeeper of Values and Decency

Company Secretaries are not only enablers of compliance - they're cultivators of governance culture.

In the boardroom, *how* decisions are made matters as much as *what* decisions are made. Company Secretaries shape this culture by working closely with leadership.

They:

- Co-create board agendas with strategy in mind
- Maintain director induction and orientation tools
- Manage the governance calendar
- Highlight regulatory changes affecting decisions

10 Quiet Influence Tools of an Effective Company Secretary

1. Strategy-Infused Agenda Planning
2. Director Orientation with Role Clarity
3. Governance Dashboards for Committee Oversight
4. Pre-Vote Briefs for the Chair

5. Highlighting Conflicts Without Conflict
6. Framing Dissent Constructively in Minutes
7. Ethical Pause Prompts Before Approvals
8. Diligent Application of Secretarial Standards
9. Documenting Rationale for Decisions
10. Respectful Board Action Follow-Up

"The Company Secretary is the invisible hand that shapes visible decisions."

Their influence is quiet but powerful. They ensure legal soundness and moral substance, and write the official memory of it all.

Pillar 3: Multi-Regulatory Mastery (FEMA, RBI, FDI, and Beyond)

From Local Compliance to Global Readiness

As businesses globalize, Company Secretaries must manage multiple legal landscapes - from FEMA and FDI to ECB, SEZ, and ODI.

Whether it's foreign remittances, regulatory approvals, or RBI interactions, the Company Secretary must connect every layer.

10 Core Multi-Regulatory Responsibilities

1. FC-GPR & FIRMS Portal Filings
2. ODI Structuring & Shareholding Approvals
3. ECB Reporting & Loan Covenant Management
4. FDI Cap Monitoring & Press Note Compliance
5. FEMA-Compliant ESOP Structuring for NRIs

6. Coordination with Authorized Dealers
7. Foreign Remittance & Valuation Reporting
8. RBI Clarification & Representation
9. FEMA-Consistent Share Transfer Compliance
10. Regulatory Sandbox Navigation for Startups

"Compliance isn't a paper trail - it's a trust trail."

The Company Secretary ensures global ambitions rest on a rock-solid regulatory base.

Not Just A Company Secretary: A Deal Enabler

Vivek, a Company Secretary at a mid-sized listed company, **was known for his governance hygiene.** When the company **sought funding from an international investor, his foresight proved critical.**

He:

- Prepared spotless compliance documentation
- Disclosed past lapses transparently
- Pre-cleared fund flows with the RBI
- Showcased rigorous audit committee documentation

An investor said:

"We trusted them because they showed us everything - even what they fixed."

His moral courage, FEMA mastery, and governance records turned a "maybe" deal into a premium close.

He wasn't just a Company Secretary - he was a deal enabler.

The Pre-Board Flight Checklist – 10 Must-Haves

1. Updated Statutory Registers
2. Timely Notice & Agenda with Notes
3. Draft Resolutions Ready
4. Director Disclosures Confirmed
5. Committee Recommendations Collated
6. CEO/CFO Certifications Secured
7. Quorum & Conflict Checks Done
8. Draft SEBI/ROC Filings Ready
9. Past Minutes Reviewed for Follow-Ups
10. Presentations and Policies Uploaded

"If the Company Secretary isn't ready, the board can't really fly."

Reminder: Technical Work = Trust Built at Scale

Most Company secretaries' work is invisible. But its outcomes - investor trust, board clarity, legal resilience - shape the company's reputation.

"Every balance sheet has numbers. A Company Secretary adds trust to them."

Boardroom Reflections – 15 Questions for Every Company Secretary

1. Am I enabling strategic decisions or just compliance checks?
2. Are my minutes a record of wisdom or just wording?

3. Do I brief the board on what they *need* to know, or what they *want* to hear?
4. Have I prepared our governance for the next crisis?
5. Do our policies reflect current law or outdated templates?
6. Are conflicts flagged proactively or reactively?
7. Do I have systems that ensure no surprises?
8. Are board decisions inclusive, ethical, and future-ready?
9. Would I trust this board based on our records?
10. Do I treat filings as sacred duties or mechanical chores?
11. Am I mentoring others to think strategically?
12. Do our disclosures reflect conscience, not just compliance?
13. Is my voice truly heard - or just documented?
14. Do I know when to speak - and when to signal instead?
15. Am I proud of the legacy I'm building in every set of minutes?

In every decision, deadline, and moral crossroad, the Company Secretary stands tall.

Not just with technical knowledge, but with an unshakable heart.

That's guardianship. That's trust built at scale. That's you.

CHAPTER 5

BEYOND THE ROLE: WHAT EVERY COMPANY SECRETARY CAN CHOOSE TO BECOME

Behind every ethical, well-run organization, there's someone quietly ensuring that the foundations are sound.

That someone is often the Company Secretary.

But in the modern world, the expectations from a CS go far beyond minutes and meetings. Today, Company Secretaries are evolving into governance leaders, strategic advisors, ethical sentinels, and drivers of responsible growth.

The real question **isn't just what you do — it's who you choose to become** within your role.

This chapter is a mirror to reflect your current self.

And it's a map to chart the identities you can adopt to grow into a leader who shapes outcomes.

Let's explore five powerful identities that every Company Secretary can intentionally build, irrespective of where they work or how senior they are.

1. **The Lifelong Learner**

   "The more you learn, the better you serve."

   No profession evolves as rapidly as compliance and governance. Laws are revised. Expectations shift. Technology redefines how we work. A CS who stands still is already falling behind.

   To thrive in this ecosystem, you must make learning a non-negotiable habit, not a once-in-a-while activity, but **a mindset of perpetual curiosity**.

What you can do

- **Update continuously**: Track amendments in the Companies Act, SEBI LODR, FEMA, and RBI circulars
- **Expand your base**: Explore ESG reporting, sustainability standards, AI, and data privacy frameworks
- **Go global**: Learn about GDPR, FCPA, and international governance codes
- **Invest in you**: Attend webinars, do short certifications, or pursue advanced courses in strategy, leadership, or public policy

When you learn consistently, two things happen:

1. You earn credibility
2. You unlock confidence to speak in any room

Insight: The boardroom listens not to the loudest voice, but to the most prepared one. Be that voice.

2. **The Ethical Compass**

   "In moments of crisis, we don't just protect the company. We protect its soul."

There will be times when your ethics are tested. A delayed disclosure. A missed compliance. A grey-zone transaction. A CEO who asks you to 'adjust' something.

In these moments, your real identity is revealed — not by the letters after your name, but by the **values** you live by.

A Company Secretary is not only the custodian of legal frameworks, but also of **organizational integrity**.

What it looks like in action

- Ensuring that internal control weaknesses are disclosed truthfully
- Pushing for timely, transparent communication with stakeholders during crises
- Advising management against decisions that are legally permissible but ethically questionable
- Keeping detailed documentation to protect the company from future scrutiny

Remember, compliance failures can hurt finances. But **ethical failures destroy trust**, and trust, once lost, is almost impossible to rebuild.

Reflection Prompt: Would you rather be popular with the management or respected by the regulators, shareholders, and your future self?

3. **The Solutionist**

"We're not the Department of No. We're the Department of How."

Let's face it — many people see Company Secretaries as gatekeepers or bottlenecks. It's time to change that narrative.

The best Company Secretary professionals don't just point out problems – they design compliant, workable solutions that support business objectives while respecting the law.

How to become a solutionist

- Learn the commercial side of every decision: Why is the company pursuing this transaction? What's the pressure behind the timeline?
- Keep a repository of past solutions and legal interpretations
- Build relationships with legal counsel, auditors, and regulators — they can often help you navigate tricky zones
- Frame every "no" as a constructive "yes, but here's how…"

  Example: Instead of saying, "You can't issue shares this way," say:

> ***"As per Sections 62 and 42, here's the compliant route. We'll need this documentation, and I'll prepare the board note by Friday."***

Result? You go from being a gatekeeper… to a go-to guide.

4. The Governance Innovator

"Governance isn't just a check-box. It's a lever for competitive advantage."

Today, investors, regulators, and stakeholders expect **good governance**, not just minimum compliance.

And in many companies, the Company Secretaries are uniquely positioned to innovate how governance is practiced.

You don't need to wait for a crisis or an audit remark to take action. You can start by **embedding governance into the DNA** of the organization.

Ways to innovate

- Propose a *Governance Dashboard* to track board actions, risks, disclosures, and sustainability metrics
- Create awareness modules for the management on insider trading, RPTs, ESG, and audit committee expectations
- Digitize board processes using secure portals, AI-minuting tools, and compliance workflows
- Advocate for board diversity, whistleblower policies, and risk heat maps

Remember, **smart governance builds long-term trust**, reduces regulatory friction, and positions the company as a responsible business.

Insight: Innovation isn't about technology alone — it's about mindset. Even a compliance calendar can be redesigned to create clarity, ownership, and accountability.

5. **The Intrapreneur**

"In a startup, governance is created from scratch. In a corporate, it's reimagined for scale."

You don't need to start your own company to think like a founder. **An intrapreneur is someone who acts like an entrepreneur within their organization** — building systems, leading change, and solving big problems.

Whether you're in a startup or a listed firm, there's always an opportunity to lead something new.

Intrapreneurial acts for a CS

- Setting up entity-wide SOPs for compliance tracking
- Spearheading a legal tech adoption project
- Leading fundraising rounds with due diligence and ROC actions
- Building investor decks for the regulatory aspects of IPOs
- Guiding the CEO and CFO on evolving ESG disclosure norms

This mindset also opens new career doors — to CXO roles, board positions, or business leadership.

Remember: Intrapreneurs don't wait for roles. They create impact, and the role follows.

CHAPTER 6

UNLOCKING GROWTH OPPORTUNITIES FOR PRACTISING COMPANY SECRETARIES

The role of the Company Secretaries has evolved far beyond routine compliance. Today's practising Company Secretaries is a governance strategist, risk guide, and entrepreneurial advisor-not just a "compliance officer." With regulators like the MCA, SEBI, and RBI reinforcing principles of transparency, stakeholder protection, and responsible governance, Company Secretaries are being recognized as essential catalysts of integrity and growth.

In practice, this means Company Secretaries must master not only the Companies Act but also an expansive legal and regulatory ecosystem-FEMA, SEBI LODR, IBC, POSH, CSR, RERA, and more. The ones who embrace this broader spectrum are unlocking immense professional and business potential.

The form-filler stereotype is long gone. The Practicing Company Secretaries today is a value-adding advisors supporting business structuring, managing legal risks, shaping board practices, and aligning business strategies with dynamic legal frameworks.

Core Practice Areas in High Demand

1. **Secretarial Audit (Section 204)**

   Mandatory for listed entities and large private companies, secretarial audit is now central to governance assurance. Practising Company Secretaries are expected not just to detect non-compliance but to interpret root causes and recommend remediation.

   Done right, a secretarial audit becomes a governance health report, not a checklist.

Pro tip: ***Strong audits build recurring mandates and deepen trust with promoters and boards.***

2. **FEMA, FDI & ECB Advisory**

   In a borderless economy, FEMA compliance is mission-critical. Practising Company Secretaries advise on:

   - Entry routes (equity, CCD, CCPS, convertible notes)
   - Sectoral caps, automatic vs. approval routes
   - FC-GPR, FLA, and ECB reporting
   - Compounding and rectification strategy

   Premium niche: One mistake can cost lakhs. Precision earns trust and long-term retainers. **3. India Entry & Foreign Subsidiary Setup**

   Foreign companies setting up in India need end-to-end guidance from structuring to RBI filings. Practising Company Secretaries provide:

- Pre-incorporation advisory (FEMA + Companies Act)
- Drafting governance frameworks (MoA, AoA, SHA)
- Filing capital inflows, reporting share allotments

Bundle with ROC, GST, and payroll to create a turnkey "India Entry Kit."

4. **Due Diligence for M&A & Fundraising**

Investors don't like surprises. Company Secretary-led diligence uncovers:

- Gaps in statutory filings or approvals
- Non-compliant board decisions
- Absence of registers or poor record-keeping
- Legal or regulatory exposure

Increasingly, Company Secretaries support deal documentation- Scheme of Arrangement, NCLT filings, and post-deal compliance.

5. **Outsourced Compliance Partner (Startups & MSMEs)**

Fast-growing companies often lack compliance capacity. Offer a monthly compliance retainer:

- Board/shareholder meeting protocols
- Checklists, templates, and filings
- Real-time dashboard reports
- Regular advisory calls

Scalable model: One Company Secretary team can handle 20+ clients using tech.

6. **Representation Before Authorities**

   Practising Company Secretaries can represent clients before:

   - **ROC:** Striking off, compounding, condonation
   - **RD:** Shifting offices, fast-track mergers
   - **NCLT:** Revival, liquidation, share capital reduction

   Drafting + representation = higher-value engagements.

Emerging Niches with Big Potential

1. **Registered Valuer (Securities/Financial Assets)**

   Under the Companies Act & IBC, valuation is now regulated. Company Secretaries can certify valuations for:

   - Fundraising & ESOPs
   - Mergers & acquisitions
   - Exit pricing for investors

   A blend of legal and financial acumen makes Company Secretaries a natural fit.

2. **Insolvency Professional (IBC)**

   With 10+ years of experience, Company Secretaries can become Resolution Professionals or Liquidators:

   - Manage corporate resolution
   - Oversee CoC and evaluate bids
   - File updates and liaise with IBBI

   Restructuring is a growing field-ideal for Company Secretaries with strategic mindset.

3. **POSH Compliance & Training**

   Companies need:

   - Written policies
   - Internal Committee setup
   - Training & awareness sessions
   - Independent inquiries

   Company Secretaries can become External Members or train Internal committee-creating trust and long-term partnerships.

4. **CSR & ESG Advisory**

   Boards need help translating compliance into impact:

   - CSR project vetting
   - Budget tracking & reporting
   - Impact analysis

   ESG is a board-level priority. Company Secretaries can evolve into ESG leads or "Sustainability Secretaries."

5. **RERA Advisory (Real Estate)**

   Builders need help navigating:

   - Project registration & compliance
   - Allotment letters & sale agreements
   - Buyer disclosures & reporting

   Tier-II cities are ripe with RERA opportunities.

Scaling Your Practice: Think Like an Entrepreneur

Build Retainer Models

- ➢ Annual compliance + audit
- ➢ Tiered retainers (Basic, Pro, Premium)
- ➢ Add "on-call" advisory or quarterly strategy calls

Productize Your Services

- **Startup Launch Kit:** Incorporation + PAN + GST + Founders Agreement + templates
- **Investor Readiness:** ROC cleanup + cap table review + legal due diligence

Leverage Technology

- Use Google Sheets/SaaS dashboards
- Automate MCA reminders
- Deploy XBRL tools & filing bots
- Use CRM for managing clients, timelines, and renewals

Build Your Digital Brand

- Post weekly LinkedIn updates
- Write Company Secretary Journal articles or blogs
- Host webinars or Q&A sessions

Create an Allied Network

- **Partner with:** CA + Lawyer + IP + Valuer
- Offer "One-Stop Compliance Hub"

Action Toolkit: Future-Proof Your Practice

1. **Pick a Niche & Upskill**: Register for a valuation, ESG, or IBC course this month.
2. **Convert 3 Clients to Retainers**: Create a pitch deck with bundled services + advisory hotline.
3. **Launch Your Online Brand**: Share compliance tips weekly. Use Canva for infographiCompany Secretary.

4. **Build a Productized Offer**: "Incorporation-to-ESOP Kit" or "POSH Policy Toolkit." Automate delivery.
5. **Form Your Dream Team:** CA + Lawyer + IP. Co-pitch as a "Governance Success Squad."

The world needs ethical advisors-not just form-fillers.

If you're a practising Company Secretary, embrace your potential. Be curious, be bold, and be entrepreneurial.

You are not just a custodian of compliance-you are a catalyst for corporate trust.

Own it. Scale it. Lead it.

Welcome to the era of Governance Entrepreneurship.

CHAPTER 7

RISING FROM WITHIN: OPPORTUNITIES FOR COMPANY SECRETARIES IN EMPLOYMENT

"A modern Company Secretary is no longer a silent scribe; they are the conscience, the navigator, and-increasingly-the strategist of the boardroom."

Why This Chapter Matters

Every day, thousands of in-house Company Secretaries walk into boardrooms with agendas and registers. But only a few walk out having influenced strategy.

This chapter is your roadmap for becoming part of that few. A blend of playbook + pep talk, it reveals:

- The evolution from compliance officer to governance leader
- High-impact roles inside corporates
- Emerging niches (ESG, AI, Dispute Resolution)
- Cross-functional leverage points

- Future-proof skills
- A real-world transformation story
- A self-check to map your growth arc

Let's begin.

From Compliance Executor to Governance Leader

Gone are the days when in-house Company Secretaries were compliance officers.

Today's boards rely on them for:

- Anticipating risks
- Aligning business with regulation
- Translating law into strategic value

The Changing Governance Perspective

Yesterday	Today
Filing officer	Governance architect
Decision recorder	Agenda shaper
Regulatory firefighter	Risk radar
Departmental silo	Cross-functional integrator

Key Expectation Shifts

- **Agenda-shaping:** Raise forward-looking topics like AI risk.
- **Stakeholder choreography:** Align board decisions with regulators, ESG raters, and investors.
- **Strategic alignment:** Bridge corporate goals and ethical expectations.

A governance leader anticipates, educates, and orchestrates.

A Unicorn Founder Applauds Company Secretaries

"As a founder scaling a company from seed to unicorn, **I've seen firsthand how invaluable a sharp Company Secretary and a strong CS Department can be.** From decoding complex investor rights during funding rounds to ensuring our boardroom is equipped for sound legal decisions, **their counsel has been the silent engine behind our governance and growth**. This book finally gives them the recognition they deserve."

Founder- Unicorn Startup

High-Impact Roles Inside the Corporate Structure

Group Company Secretary

- Standardizes governance across 10–100+ group entities
- Centralizes filings, calendars, and ESG protocols

Outcome: Fewer penalties. Faster board actions.

Head of Legal & Compliance / CGO

- Merges secretarial, legal, ethiCompany Secretary, and risk under one umbrella
- Reports directly to the CEO or the Board

Outcome: Seat at the strategic table.

IPOs & M&A Governance Lead

- Orchestrates due diligence, disclosures, and investor documents
- Keeps the board aligned with deal timelines

Outcome: High visibility = faster career lift.

Regulator Liaison / Nodal Officer

- Acts as the face of the company to SEBI/MCA/RBI
- Drives a proactive compliance culture

Outcome: Trust capital with regulators.

ESG & Stakeholder Engagement Officer

- Owns BRSR, GRI, and global sustainability reporting
- Aligns ESG data with investor storytelling

Outcome: Boardroom credibility + investor appeal

Ethics & Whistleblower Framework Advisor

- Crafts Codes of Conduct, incident dashboards
- Ensures early fraud detection and resolution

Outcome: Culture of trust and transparency

Strategic Niches to Watch

Corporate Arbitrator

- Drafts arbitration frameworks
- Avoids costly litigation

Compliance Risk Architect

- Builds risk heat maps, real-time dashboards
- Embeds governance into SOPs

Board Process Innovator

- Champions digital tools, board portals
- Accelerates meeting prep & decision cycles

Policy Shaper & Culture Custodian

- Leads DEI, AI-ethiCompany Secretary, and cyber governance
- Bridges HR, brand, and board values

The Cross-Functional Influence Map

Function	Collaboration Touchpoints	Company Secretary Value-Addition
Finance	Reports, Decks	Align the story with financial metriCompany Secretary
Legal	Contracts, Litigation	Add compliance foresight
HR	POSH, Ethics	Guide tone-from-the-top
IT/Data	Privacy, AI	Translate risk into governance action
ESG/ Sustainability	KPIs, Disclosures	Align with investor-grade sustainability goals

Break silos. Multiply your value.

Future-Proof Your Skills (2025 → 2030)

Skill	Why It Matters	How to Master
Boardroom Storytelling	Directors need clarity, not clauses	Toastmasters, storytelling workshops
Data Privacy Fluency	DPDP/GDPR defines a license to operate	ICSI certifications

ESG Frameworks	ESG now shapes investment choices	IFRS-ISSB, GRI training
Arbitration Skills	Save time, money in disputes	Arbitration centres (NPAC, ICA)
Tech Governance	Boards fear AI risks	MIT/Stanford online courses, internal committees
Public Affairs Savvy	Regulations are policy outcomes	Business diplomacy programs
Design Thinking	Solve complex problems creatively	IDEO U, LinkedIn Learning

Your Career Acceleration Playbook

Here are some exciting ways that you can take & establish governance initiatives and credibility.

- **Pitch a Board-level Project:** AI risk register, ESG dashboard, or board portal rollout.
- **Shadow a CXO:** Quarterly mentoring lunch with CFO/GC.
- **Publish & Present:** Speak on webinars, write insights.
- **Mentor & Build a Bench:** Prove leadership through succession.
- **Strategic Reporting:** Own sections of annual report narratives.
- **Join Internal Committees:** ESG, ethics, and risk. Exposure = trust.

Your Self-Assessment Grid

You can only correct what you can identify; self-awareness is the key to improvement. Use the questions given below to review and improve your contribution, presentation, and value.

Question

- Do I brief the board on new risks (AI, climate, cyber)?
- Have I led a cross-functional governance initiative this year?
- Do I maintain non-transactional rapport with regulators?
- Can I articulate our business model, ESG position, and top risks?
- Have I published or presented externally in the last 6 months?
- Am I mentoring junior Company Secretaries or sharing knowledge internally?

Scoring & Interpretation

For each yes, give yourself one point.

- Score 5–6 Yes → You're flying.
- Score 3–4 Yes → Growing focus, upskill.
- Score 0–2 Yes → Start now. Start small.

Your business card may still say *Company Secretary*. But in the board's eyes, you are the *Strategic Conscience*.

Boards crave foresight. Regulators demand ethics. Teams look for clarity.

Step up. Speak up. Shape more than minutes-shape futures.

"Compliance records the past; governance designs the future. Design boldly."

CHAPTER 8

CONCLUSION – CONTINUING THE JOURNEY

TAKE PRIDE IN HOW FAR YOU'VE COME

As we close this book, pause for a moment. Reflect not just on the facts, forms, or filing requirements, but on something deeper. You've explored what it truly means to be a Company Secretary in today's dynamic, high-stakes world. You've journeyed through the roots of this noble profession and glimpsed its limitless potential.

This is no small feat. From the Companies Act and FEMA to boardroom dynamiCompany Secretary, and emerging governance challenges, you've walked a path that demands intellectual rigor, emotional intelligence, and ethical fortitude. Few professions blend technical mastery and moral leadership like this one.

So yes, stand tall. Your role matters more than ever.

As the world leans into sustainability, transparency, and stakeholder trust, the Company Secretary is no longer just relevant-they're essential. You are the invisible force holding the visible world of business together.

You've learned how a Company Secretary:

- Ensures regulatory excellence
- Bridges, boards, and stakeholders
- Upholds fairness, accountability, and transparency
- Enables ethical, strategic business choices

Every resolution you draft is part of India's corporate architecture. Every filing you deliver builds investor confidence. Every stand you take cements the moral spine of industry.

Remember that first rush of pride when you cleared your Company Secretary exams? That wasn't the finish line-it was the beginning of a life of purpose.

You Are Not Just a Company Secretary – You Are a Guardian of Governance

For too long, the word "secretary" has been underestimated. But let's set the record straight:

You don't just ensure compliance. You shape policy. You guide leaders through legal fog. You keep organizations aligned with their values.

Every time you:

- Interpret the law into action
- Counsel boards on ethical risks
- Spot gaps in transparency
- Document decisions with foresight

You're **safeguarding integrity.**

The Company Secretary has rightly been called the "guardian of good corporate governance."

This isn't ceremonial. It reflects:

- Your vigilance on compliance
- Your voice of conscience in the boardroom
- Your stewardship of internal governance systems

Wikipedia sums it up well:

> ***The Company Secretary is a "facilitator between board and stakeholders, guardian of records, and gatekeeper of legal and ethical obligations."***

As governance becomes the foundation of sustainable capitalism, your expertise becomes the cornerstone of trust. Whether in MNCompany Secretary or startups, you carry the torch of clarity and conscience.

You are not a box-ticker. You are the compass.

Mentor, Learn, Contribute: Grow Together

This profession isn't a solo journey. It's a collective legacy-a community that uplifts, shares, and strengthens.

Mentor and Guide

We all remember the person who explained that tricky provision before exams, or calmed our nerves before our first AGM.

Now it's your turn.

- Mentor students or interns
- Share your journey at ICompany SecretaryI events
- Join formal mentorship programs

Mentoring deepens your wisdom and lights the path for others.

"When you mentor someone, you multiply your impact."

Embrace Lifelong Learning

In this era of change, stagnation is regression.

Tomorrow's Company Secretary must be:

- Technologically empowered
- ESG-savvy
- Globally fluent

So:

- Read that journal
- Join that webinar
- Take that new course

Knowledge is not optional-it's your superpower.

Share Your Expertise

Your experience is valuable. Let it speak.

- Write for the Company Secretary Journal
- Post regulatory insights on LinkedIn
- Start a blog on practical governance

Visibility is not vanity-it's contribution.

Build Stronger Networks

Good governance thrives in good company.

- Attend ICSI events
- Join digital Company Secretary communities
- Collaborate on webinars, study groups

"When one of us grows, all of us rise."

I Walk With You

I'm **CS Dikshant Malhotra**, Fellow Company Secretary, founder of **Dikshant Malhotra & Associates,** a decade-old firm based in Gurugram serving startups, corporates, and MNCs in matters of Company Law, FEMA, SEBI, and Business Governance.

I began my journey like many of you-filled with questions, driven by purpose. I remember:

- Handling Clients' Objections
- Filing MCA forms under deadline pressure
- Watching governance shift from registers to dashboards

I've made mistakes. I've learned. I've taught. And most importantly, I've walked the same path you're walking now.

Today, I lead a team of 10+ professionals, guide corporate boards, and contribute to governance conversations nationwide. But my core identity remains unchanged:

I am a proud Company Secretary-and I walk with you.

Invitation: Keep the Flame Burning

This is your second chapter-the real-world one.

Attend ICSI Events

Stay current. Learn from peers. Meet thought leaders. One event can spark your next leap.

Join Webinars & Online Platforms

- Use ICSI's portal
- Follow legal forums and SEBI briefings
- Make weekly learning a habit

Share What You Know

- Contribute to journals or blogs
- Post digestible updates online

Teaching is the highest form of mastery.

Volunteer Locally

- Lead a session at your chapter
- Organize a governance bootcamp
- Speak to students or new entrants

"If you know one thing more than someone else, you can teach."

Stay Connected

Join WhatsApp/Telegram/LinkedIn groups. These are the new-era study circles.

Closing Words: This Is Your Moment

Dear professional, dear guardian of governance-thank you.

Thank you for choosing governance. For striving. For believing in what's right.

Remember:

- Your work is meaningful
- Your voice is powerful
- Your ethics are timeless

Governance is not paperwork-it's trust. And you are its keeper.

"Speak the truth. Abide by the law." – Motto of ICSI

India is rising. Its economy is expanding, and Company Secretaries like you are the unseen architects keeping that growth ethical and enduring.

Let's move forward together.

The best is yet to come.

Let's Stay Connected

If this book resonated with you—if it sparked an idea, answered a doubt, or reignited your purpose—I'd love to hear from you.

Whether you're a Practising Company Secretary, an in-house professional, a student, or a corporate decision-maker, let's keep this conversation going beyond the pages.

Here's How You Can Reach Me:

- **Email**: cs@dmassociates.in
- **LinkedIn**: linkedin.com/in/csdikshantmalhotra
- **Website**: www.dmassociates.in

Let's Collaborate:

- Invite me to speak at your college, corporate, or CS chapter event
- Share your journey and challenges—I'm always learning from fellow professionals

The Company Secretary community thrives when we share, support, and grow together. Let's be the reason good governance rises one leader at a time.